20 Answers

&

The Papacy

Jim Blackburn

Catholic
Answers
Press

20 Answers: The Papacy

Jim Blackburn

© 2015 Catholic Answers

Published by Catholic Answers, Inc.

2020 Gillespie Way

El Cajon, California 92020

1-888-291-8000 orders

619-387-0042 fax

catholic.com

Printed in the United States of America

978-1-941663-32-5

978-1-941663-33-2 Kindle

978-1-941663-34-9 ePub

Introduction

When St. Paul evangelized in Antioch, a dispute arose among the disciples there about whether or not Gentile converts to Christianity needed to keep the Mosaic Law. Jewish converts in the community unnecessarily continued to follow precepts of the old law and they expected Gentile converts to do the same. In Acts 15, Luke relates the story of how Paul went about settling this dispute: he took the matter to the most authoritative teacher of the Faith, Peter, and the apostles in communion with him. This made perfect sense, as Jesus had long ago singled out Peter as head of the apostles, giving him unique authority in the Church (see Matt. 16:18–19).

Down through the centuries, there have been twenty-one ecumenical councils at which the apostles' successors have met under the authority of Peter's successor to definitively settle matters of faith and morals. Peter's successor—the pope, as he has come to be known—continues to be recognized as the highest teaching authority in the Church. At least this is the case for Catholics—not so among other Christians.

Unfortunately, this rejection of papal authority has resulted in widespread disunity among Christians throughout the world. Literally thousands of Christian denominations have arisen in just the last 500 years since the advent of Protestantism. Such division is a terrible breakdown in the *oneness* that Jesus intended his followers to maintain (see John 17:20–22).

Christ's followers today are splintered in so many directions that the Catholic Church itself—the one Church founded by Christ—is often mistaken among the many other Christian communities throughout the world as simply another "denomination." Disputes outside the Church over matters of faith and morals are either settled according to the fallible judgment of denomination leaders or they result in further splintering into yet countless additional sects.

Outside the Christian community, as modern culture increasingly bucks authority, the papacy has become a target of disdain. The moral decay of society is considered "progress," while the constant teachings of the Catholic Church are viewed as anything from archaic and oppressive to hateful and bigoted. The pope is a favorite bull's-eye for such attacks.

Considering the vast misunderstanding of—and disrespect toward—the papacy today, many questions need to be addressed in defense of this sacred office instituted by Christ. It is my hope that this booklet will, in however small a way, be a useful instrument in explaining and defending the papacy among the challenges it faces in the world today. In doing so, may it especially foster unity among the Christian faithful as one flock under one shepherd (John 10:16).

1. What is the papacy?

The papacy is the office and jurisdiction of the pope as the head of Christ's Church on earth. The English word "papacy" translates from the Latin word *papatus*, which derives from the Latin word *papa,* from which we get "pope." Going back even further, the Latin term *papa* comes from the Greek word *papas,* which means "father." In a real sense, the pope is like a father (that is, "papa") to the Christian faithful.

Other terms refer to the pope in his office of the papacy as well. Some examples are "bishop of Rome," "Peter's successor," "Roman pontiff," and "vicar of Christ." As the head of Christ's Church on earth, the pope is responsible for seeing that the bishops and their flocks throughout the world are unified, just as Jesus prayed for at the Last Supper (John 17:9–11):

> I am praying for them; I am not praying for the world, but for those whom thou hast given me, for they are thine; all mine are thine, and thine are mine, and I am glorified in them. And now I am no more in the world, but they are in the world, and I am coming to thee. Holy Father, keep them in thy name, which thou hast given me; that they may be one, even as we are one.

Jesus founded one Church to endure until he comes again: "I will build my church, and the powers of death shall not prevail against it" (Matt. 16:18). He uniquely empowered the papacy, with Peter as the first pope, to help ensure the unity of his one Church. The *Catechism of the Catholic Church* (CCC) explains further:

> The *pope*, bishop of Rome and Peter's successor, is the perpetual and visible source and foundation of the unity both of the bishops and of the whole company of the faithful. For the Roman Pontiff, by reason of his office as Vicar of Christ, and as pastor of the entire Church has full, supreme, and universal power over the whole Church, a power which he can always exercise unhindered. (CCC 882)

The Church recognizes that this authority comes from God: "The pope enjoys, by divine institution, 'supreme, full, immediate, and universal power in the care of souls'" (CCC 937).

At the time of this writing, Pope Francis is the current pope. St. Peter was the first pope and there have been a total of 267 down through the history of the Church. This is not a fact that must be taken on faith; as we will see, it is documented historically.

No other church can lay claim to the unique leadership with which Jesus endowed his one true Church, the Catholic Church, for the sake of unity in doctrine and practice.

2. Why does the Church need the papacy? Can't we just follow Jesus?

In order for Christ's Church to be unified as he prayed it would be, Jesus established a hierarchical authority with one person at the head, so that we could be sure that in following that person we would be following him. It makes sense for there to be such a single authority overseeing the Church throughout the world; to govern it, sanctify it, and perhaps most importantly, to ensure that it continue to teach Christ's truth in its fullness, free from corruption, down through the ages. This teaching authority is called the *Magisterium*, and it comprises the pope (at its head) and all the bishops in communion with him.

In the first century St. Peter wrote, "There are some things in [Paul's letters] hard to understand, which the ignorant and unstable twist to their own destruction, as they do the other scriptures" (2 Pet. 3:16). Here we see that even during the apostolic age there was concern about misguided interpretations of Scripture. Sacred Tradition could easily be corrupted as well. Peter went on to warn Christians, "You therefore, beloved, knowing this beforehand, beware lest you be carried away with the error of lawless men and lose your own stability" (2 Pet. 3:17).

How were early Christians to know who was teaching the truth? Not all the many different interpretations of Scripture and prophecies they were hearing could be correct. There must have been some way that they could discern who was teaching Christ's truth and who was misguiding them. Of course, this is why Jesus gave certain disciples authority to teach in his name. The early Christians knew they could trust Peter's teaching because he was the head of Jesus' apostles, those disciples who Jesus first appointed with everlasting authority to teach.

At the Last Supper, Jesus promised the apostles that the Father "will give you another Counselor, to be with you forever . . . the Holy Spirit, whom the Father will send in my name, he will teach you all things, and bring to your remembrance all that I have said to you . . . he will guide you into all the truth" (John 14:16, 26; 16:13).

Later, before his Ascension, Jesus instructed Peter and the apostles: "Go therefore and make disciples of all nations, baptizing them in the name of the Father and of the Son and of the Holy Spirit, teaching them to observe all that I have commanded you; and lo, I am with you always, to the close of the age" (Matt. 28:19–20). This *Great Commission* was to be carried out in Jesus' absence, after the Ascension, under the guidance of the Holy Spirit.

The promise of the Holy Spirit's coming was fulfilled in a special way at Pentecost:

When the day of Pentecost had come, they were all together in one place. And suddenly a sound came from heaven like the rush of a mighty wind, and it filled all the house where they were sitting. And there appeared to them tongues as of fire, distributed and resting on each one of them. And they were all filled with the Holy Spirit and began to speak in other tongues, as the Spirit gave them utterance. (Acts 2:1–4)

Thus, the Holy Spirit came upon the Magisterium (Peter and the other apostles, the first bishops) as Jesus promised, and he continues to guide it today. With the Holy Spirit's guidance, the Church's teaching authority remains true to Jesus and his teachings.

The Roman Pontiff and the bishops are "authentic teachers, that is, teachers endowed with the authority of Christ, who preach the faith to the people entrusted to them, the faith to be believed and put into practice." The *ordinary* and universal *Magisterium* of the pope and the bishops in communion with him teach the faithful the truth to believe, the charity to practice, the beatitude to hope for (CCC 2034).

"The task of giving an authentic interpretation of the Word of God, whether in its written form or in the form of Tradition, has been entrusted to the living teaching office of the Church alone. Its authority in this matter is exercised in the name of Jesus Christ." This means that the task of interpretation has been entrusted to the bishops in communion with the successor of Peter, the bishop of Rome. (CCC 85)

3. Where in the Bible is the papacy mentioned?

Keep in mind that not everything that is true must be mentioned in the Bible. St. John the Evangelist wrote, "Now Jesus did many other signs in the presence of the disciples, which are not written in this book; but these are written that you may believe that Jesus is the Christ, the Son of God, and that believing you may have life in his name. . . . there are also many other things which Jesus did; were every one of them to be written, I suppose that the world itself could not contain the books that would be written" (John 20:30–31; 21:25).

Even so, we do find the pope and his office mentioned in the Bible. The terms "pope" and "papacy" were not yet being used when the New Testament was written—those terms would come into use later—but the office and authority had already been established and we find their foundation on the lips of Jesus.

First, Jesus set apart twelve of his disciples and made them apostles. The word "apostle" comes from the Greek word *apostolos,* which denotes one who is sent as a messenger. Early Christians recognized that St. Peter and the apostles were indeed sent by Christ and endowed with special authority to teach in his name. St. Luke records Jesus appointing the Twelve (Luke 6:13–17; see also Matt. 10:2–4):

And when it was day, he called his disciples, and chose from them twelve, whom he named apostles; Simon, whom he named Peter, and Andrew his brother, and James, and John, and Philip, and Bartholomew, and Matthew, and Thomas, and James the son of Alphaeus, and Simon who was called the Zealot, and Judas the son of James [also known as Thaddaeus], and Judas Iscariot, who became a traitor.

St. Matthew tells us how Jesus later singled out Peter from among the apostles to be his first disciple with the authority of the papacy:

Now when Jesus came into the district of Caesarea Philippi, he asked his disciples, "Who do men say that the Son of man is?" And they said, "Some say John the Baptist, others say Elijah, and others Jeremiah or one of the prophets." He said to them, "But who do you say that I am?" Simon Peter replied, "You are the Christ, the Son of the living God." And Jesus answered him, "Blessed are you, Simon Bar-Jona! For flesh and blood has not revealed this to you, but my Father who is in heaven. And I tell you, you are Peter, and on this rock I will build my church, and the powers of death shall not prevail against it. I will give you the keys of the kingdom of heaven, and whatever you bind on earth shall be bound in heaven, and whatever you loose on earth shall be loosed in heaven." (Matt. 16:13–19)

Thus, Peter was specially chosen from among the apostles and promised special authority not given to others. Later, after the Resurrection but before his Ascension, Jesus reaffirmed Peter's role as the first pope:

When they had finished breakfast, Jesus said to Simon Peter, "Simon, son of John, do you love me more than these?" He said to him, "Yes, Lord; you know that I love you." He said to him, "Feed my lambs." A second time he said to him, "Simon, son of John, do you love me?" He said to him, "Yes, Lord; you know that I love you." He said to him, "Tend my sheep." He said to him the third time, "Simon, son of John, do you love me?" Peter was grieved because he said to him the third time, "Do you love me?" And he said to him, "Lord, you know everything; you know that I love you." Jesus said to him, "Feed my sheep. Truly, truly, I say to you, when you were young, you girded yourself and walked where you would; but when you are old, you will stretch out your hands, and another will gird you and carry you where you do not wish to go." (This he said to show by what death he was to glorify God.) And after this he said to him, "Follow me." (John 21:15–19)

Many scholars see in this passage a threefold reaffirmation of Peter's special authority after he had denied Jesus three times (see John 18:15–18, 25–27).

Thus, we do find in the Bible that Jesus appointed twelve of his disciples to be apostles and, from among them, he elevated Peter, the "rock," as their head. Peter and the apostles later went on to appoint successors to carry on their work and further it after their deaths. These successors were the first bishops of the Church, and the successors to Peter's office as head of the apostles were the earliest popes. This arrangement helped to assure the unity that Jesus prayed for.

> When Christ instituted the Twelve, "he constituted them in the form of a college or permanent assembly, at the head of which he placed Peter, chosen from among them." Just as "by the Lord's institution, St. Peter and the rest of the apostles constitute a single apostolic college, so in like fashion the Roman Pontiff, Peter's successor, and the bishops, the successors of the apostles, are related with and united to one another." (CCC 880)

4. Did Christians in the early Church understand Peter to be the "rock" in the same way Catholics do today?

Some Christians argue that Jesus did not build his Church with Peter as its head (that is, "rock") but with something else at its foundation, such as Peter's proclamation that Jesus is the Christ or, more simply, Peter's strong faith. This being the case, it is important to discover what the earliest Christians understood the "rock" of Matthew 16 to be.

Many bishops and other Christians who were contemporaries of the apostles or who lived in the centuries after them continued to write books and letters similar to those in the New Testament (though not inspired by the Holy Spirit as Scripture is). Many of these have been preserved and come down to us through history. These writings of the early Church Fathers provide insight into what the Christians of the first few centuries believed. Many of these writers were bishops, and thus part of the Magisterium headed by Peter's successor. Passages from several of their writings do, indeed, confirm that from the earliest centuries of the Church the "rock" was understood to be Peter:

Tertullian (A.D. 200): "Was anything withheld from the knowledge of Peter, who is called 'the rock on which the Church would be built' with the power of 'loosing and binding in heaven and on earth'?"[1]

Tertullian (220): "What kind of man are you, subverting and changing what was the manifest intent of the Lord when he conferred this personally upon

Peter? Upon *you*, he says, I will build my Church; and I will give to *you* the keys."[2]

Letter of Clement to James (221): "Be it known to you, my lord, that Simon [Peter], who, for the sake of the true faith, and the most sure foundation of his doctrine, was set apart to be the foundation of the Church, and for this end was by Jesus himself, with his truthful mouth, named Peter."[3]

Clementine Homilies (221): "[Simon Peter said to Simon Magus in Rome:] 'For you now stand in direct opposition to me, who am a firm rock, the foundation of the Church.'"[4]

Origen (248): "Look at [Peter], the great foundation of the Church, that most solid of rocks, upon whom Christ built the Church."[5]

Cyprian of Carthage (251): "On him [Peter] he builds the Church, and to him he gives the command to feed the sheep [John 21:17], and although he assigns a like power to all the apostles, yet he founded a single chair [*cathedra*], and he established by his own authority a source and an intrinsic reason for that unity. Indeed, the others were that also which Peter was [apostles], but a primacy is given to Peter, whereby it is made clear that there is but one Church and one chair. . . . If someone does not hold fast to this unity of Peter, can he imagine that he still holds the faith? If he [should] desert the chair of Peter upon whom the Church was built, can he still be confident that he is in the Church?"[6]

Cyprian (253): "There is one God and one Christ, and one Church, and one chair founded on Peter by the word of the Lord. It is not possible to set up another altar or for there to be another priesthood besides that one altar and that one priesthood. Whoever has gathered elsewhere is scattering."[7]

"There [John 6:68–69] speaks Peter, upon whom the Church would be built, teaching in the name of the Church and showing that even if a stubborn and proud multitude withdraws because it does not wish to obey, yet the Church does not withdraw from Christ."[8]

Firmilian (c. 253): "[Pope] Stephen [I] . . . boasts of the place of his episcopate, and contends that he holds the succession from Peter, on whom the foundations of the Church were laid."[9]

Ephraim the Syrian (351): "[Jesus said:] 'Simon, my follower, I have made you the foundation of the holy Church. I betimes called you Peter, because you will support all its buildings. You are the inspector of those who will build on earth a Church for me. If they should wish to build what is false, you, the foundation, will condemn them. You are the head of the fountain from which my teaching flows; you are the chief of my disciples.'"[10]

Optatus (367): "You cannot deny that you are aware that in the city of Rome the episcopal chair was given first to Peter; the chair in which Peter sat, the same who was head—that is why he is also called Cephas

['Rock']—of all the apostles; the one chair in which unity is maintained by all."[11]

Ambrose of Milan (379): "Could [Christ] not, then, strengthen the faith of the man to whom, acting on his own authority, he gave the kingdom, whom he called the rock, thereby declaring him to be the foundation of the Church?"[12]

Jerome (393): "[O]ne among the twelve is chosen to be their head in order to remove any occasion for division."[13]

These and other examples that could be cited leave no doubt that from its earliest years the Church understood Jesus' words to Peter in Matthew 16 to affirm that Peter himself is the "rock" upon which Jesus built his Church.

5. Catholics claim that Peter served his papacy as the first bishop of Rome. But doesn't the Bible say he was never there, since Paul, writing from Rome, says, "Only Luke is with me" (2 Tim. 4:11)?

This is a common challenge posed by non-Catholics. If Peter was never in Rome, it goes, he could not have been Rome's first bishop and so could not have been the first pope. How can Catholics talk about the divine origin of the papacy if our claim about Peter's whereabouts is wrong?

Fortunately, the most that 2 Timothy 4:11 could prove is that Peter was not in Rome at the time Paul was writing. It does not prove that Peter was never there, only that he was somewhere else at that time. We should not read more into a verse than is warranted. After all, if we were to follow the line of reasoning in this objection strictly, we would have to conclude that *no other Christians at all* were in Rome, other than Paul and Luke. But, of course, we know that Rome had a large Christian community.

Moreover, the Bible does allude to Peter being in Rome. Peter concludes his first epistle with a cryptic greeting from "Babylon." This doesn't refer to the Mesopotamian city that figures so prominently in the Old Testament. Rather, it was the early Church's code word for Rome, chosen because the Romans were persecuting Christians just as the Babylonians had done to the Jews. Because the Roman authorities were hunting for them, and Christians never knew when one of their letters would fall into the wrong hands, they used code words so as not to advertise their whereabouts to their persecutors. The early Christians would write in their letters, "I am in Babylon" instead of "I am in Rome."

Additionally, archaeological evidence discovered in the middle decades of the twentieth century confirms that Peter was in Rome. Researchers conducted digs under St. Peter's Basilica to verify or disprove the tradition that the basilica had been constructed over Peter's tomb. They did find his tomb, as well as neighboring crypts on which were written things like "Buried near Peter."

Thus, there is ample biblical as well as archeological evidence to prove that Peter was, indeed, stationed in Rome. Since he carried on the work of the first pope from there, it is quite natural to title his papal successor the bishop of Rome.

6. Did the early Christians say that Peter lived in Rome?

If Peter had indeed been stationed in Rome, it would make sense for early Christian writers to have attested to that fact. And when we look to the writings of the Church Fathers, we indeed find them confirming what the Catholic Church says about Peter's Roman episcopacy. In fact, not only do they indicate that Peter was in Rome, but they also indicate that *his successors* carried out their papacies from Rome as well, thus maintaining the primacy of the office of bishop of Rome.

Irenaeus (A.D. 189): "The blessed apostles [Peter and Paul], having founded and built up the church [of Rome]."[14]

Tertullian (200): "...the church of the Romans, where Clement was ordained by Peter."[15]

The Little Labyrinth (211): "Victor . . . was the thirteenth bishop of Rome from Peter."[16]

Cyprian of Carthage (253): "With a false bishop appointed for themselves by heretics, they dare even to set sail and carry letters from schismatics and blasphemers to the chair of Peter and to the principal church [at Rome], in which sacerdotal unity has its source."[17]

Eusebius of Caesarea (312): "Paul testifies that Crescens was sent to Gaul, but Linus, whom he mentions in the Second Epistle to Timothy as his companion at Rome, was Peter's successor in the episcopate of the church there . . . Clement also, who was appointed third bishop of the church at Rome, was, as Paul testifies, his co-laborer and fellow-soldier."[18]

Optatus (367): "You cannot deny that you are aware that in the city of Rome the episcopal chair was given first to Peter; the chair in which Peter sat, the same who was head—that is why he is also called Cephas [Rock]—of all the apostles; the one chair in which unity is maintained by all."[19]

Epiphanius of Salamis (375): "At Rome the first apostles and bishops were Peter and Paul, then Linus, then Cletus, then Clement, the contemporary of Peter and Paul."[20]

Pope Damasus I (382): "[T]he holy Roman Church has been placed at the forefront not by the conciliar decisions of other churches, but has received the primacy by the evangelic voice of our Lord and Savior . . . The first see [today], therefore, is that of Peter the apostle, that of the Roman Church."[21]

Jerome (383): "[Pope] Stephen . . . was the blessed Peter's twenty-second successor in the See of Rome."[22]

Augustine (402): "[W]hat has the chair of the Roman church done to you, in which Peter sat, and in which Anastasius sits today?"[23]

Peter Chrysologus (449): "We exhort you in every respect, honorable brother, to heed obediently what has been written by the most blessed pope of the city of Rome, for blessed Peter, who lives and presides in his own see, provides the truth of faith to those who seek it. For we, by reason of our pursuit of peace and faith, cannot try cases on the faith without the consent of the bishop of Rome."[24]

Clearly, Peter carried out his papacy in Rome, as his successors have continued to do from the earliest days of the Church!

7. What other scriptural evidence is there that Peter was the head of the apostles?

As we have seen, Scripture clearly shows that Jesus appointed Peter as the head of the apostles and rock of the Church. Apart from that, there is ample other evidence in the New Testament that Peter was thereafter recognized as the first in authority among the apostles.

Whenever the apostles are named, Peter is always at the head of the list. The authors of all three synoptic Gospels (Matthew, Mark, and Luke) affirm Peter's primacy in this way. Note that although the order of the Twelve varies somewhat in each account, Peter in his primacy is always listed first, while Judas in his disgrace is always listed last:

And he called to him his twelve disciples and gave them authority over unclean spirits, to cast them out, and to heal every disease and every infirmity. The names of the twelve apostles are these: first, Simon, who is called Peter, and Andrew his brother; James the son of Zebedee, and John his brother; Philip and Bartholomew; Thomas and Matthew the tax collector; James the son of Alphaeus, and Thaddaeus; Simon the Cananaean, and Judas Iscariot, who betrayed him. (Matt. 10:1–4)

And he appointed twelve, to be with him, and to be sent out to preach and have authority to cast out demons: Simon, whom he surnamed Peter; James the son of Zebedee and John the brother of James, whom he surnamed Boanerges, that is, sons of thunder; Andrew, and Philip, and Bartholomew, and Matthew, and Thomas, and James the son of Alphaeus, and Thaddaeus, and Simon the Cananaean, and Judas Iscariot, who betrayed him. (Mark 3:14–19)

And when it was day, he called his disciples, and chose from them twelve, whom he named apostles; Simon, whom he named Peter, and Andrew his brother, and James and John, and Philip, and Bartholomew, and Matthew, and Thomas, and James the son of Alphaeus, and Simon, who was called the Zealot, and Judas the son of James [also known as Thaddaeus], and Judas Iscariot, who became a traitor. (Luke 6:13–17)

Additionally, sometimes Scripture (e.g., Luke 9:32) refers to an entire group of apostles simply as "Peter and those who were with him," always naming Peter, the primary apostle, but not the others.

We also find that Peter is the one who generally speaks for all of the apostles as a group. For example, in Jesus' fourth discourse recounted by Matthew, only Peter is named: "At that time the disciples came to Jesus . . . Then Peter came up and said to him, 'Lord, how often shall my brother sin against me, and I forgive him? As many as seven times?' Jesus said to him, 'I do not say to you seven times, but seventy times seven'" (Matt. 18:1, 21–22). Note that Peter's question here concerns forgiveness, one of the primary functions of binding and loosing, which had not yet been endowed upon the other apostles. Similarly, Luke records Peter asking Jesus about a parable concerning leadership and responsibility: "Peter said, '"Lord, are you telling this parable for us or for all?"'" (Luke 12:41).

After Jesus' Bread of Life discourse in John's Gospel, Peter affirms the apostles' faith in him: "After this many of his disciples drew back and no longer went about with him. Jesus said to the twelve, 'Do you also wish to go away?' Simon Peter answered him, 'Lord, to whom shall we go? You have the words of eternal life; and we have believed, and have come to know, that you are the Holy One of God'" (John 6:66–69).

The biblical evidence for Peter's primacy doesn't end there:

- When Jesus walks on the sea, it is Peter who walks toward him on the water (Matt. 14:22–32).

- On the mount of the Transfiguration, it is Peter who acts on behalf of the apostles there (Matt. 17:1–8).

- At Pentecost it was Peter who first preached to the crowds (Acts 2:14–40), and he worked the first healing in the Church age (Acts 3:6–7).

- It is Peter's faith that will strengthen his brethren (Luke 22:32), and Peter is given Christ's flock to shepherd (John 21:17).

- An angel was sent to announce the Resurrection to Peter (Mark 16:7), and the risen Christ first appeared to Peter (Luke 24:34).

- Peter headed the meeting that elected Matthias to replace Judas (Acts 1:15–26), and he received the first converts (Acts 2:41).

- Peter inflicted the first punishment (Acts 5:1–11), and excommunicated the first heretic (Acts 8:18–23).

- Peter led the first Church council, in Jerusalem (Acts 15), and announced the first dogmatic decision (Acts 15:7–11).

- It was to Peter that the revelation came that Gentiles were to be baptized and accepted as Christians (Acts 10:46–48).

The New Testament authors clearly single Peter out as the primary and most prominent apostle.

8. Peter humbly referred to himself as only a "fellow elder" (1 Pet. 5:1). Doesn't this indicate that he didn't see himself as having any "primacy" in the Church?

As is almost always the case when interpreting Scripture, in this verse it's important to have context. Here Peter is exhorting Christians to practice the virtue of humility. A few verses later we read, "[C]lothe yourselves, all of you, with humility toward one another, for 'God opposes the proud, but gives grace to the humble.' Humble yourselves therefore under the mighty hand of God, that he may exalt you" (1 Pet. 5:5–6).

By humbly calling himself a "fellow elder," Peter is not implying that he is merely equal in authority to other Church leaders; rather, he is practicing what he preaches. Jesus calls on all Christians to practice this very kind of self-effacement, the virtue of humility: "[W]hoever would be great among you must be your servant, and whoever would be first among you must be your slave" (Matt. 20:26–27).

Peter elsewhere reminds his readers that he is an "apostle of Jesus Christ" (1 Pet. 1:1) and as such has authority to preach and teach in the name of the Lord (see Luke 10:16). The very fact that Peter sent his epistles to instruct and guide the Church shows that Peter knew he possessed an authority above that of others. Referring to himself in humble terms doesn't change that.

This sort of humility is evident throughout the apostolic writings. The lowest level of priestly minister was the deacon (sometimes called "servant" or "minister" in Scripture. The apostles ordained men to this office originally to distribute food to the needy and to wait on tables (Acts 6:1–6). Yet Paul, one of the greatest apostles and author of about half of the New Testament, describes himself in such lowly terms on several occasions (1 Cor. 3:5, 4:1; 2 Cor. 3:6, 6:4, 11:23; Eph. 3:7; Col. 1:23, 25).

If we were to claim that Peter's use of humble terms about himself meant that he had no special authority above other Christians, we would be forced to conclude, likewise, that Paul was a mere servant and therefore had no authority over other Christians. But nobody would make such a patently unbiblical assertion.

Paul, like Peter, presents himself in a humble, unassuming way—"I am the least of the apostles, unfit to be called an apostle, because I persecuted the church of God" (1 Cor. 15:9), "[T]hough I am the very least of all the saints, this grace was given" (Eph. 3:8)—but such humility does not indicate that Paul did not have jurisdiction over others. After all, he said rather pointedly, "Accordingly, though I am bold enough in Christ to command you to do what is required, yet for love's sake I prefer to appeal to you" (Philem. 8–9). Only people in authority can issue orders.

Thus, Peter's humility is an indicator of his great leadership, not evidence contrary to his papacy.

Some might here object that the papacy has not always historically appeared to be a humble office. Popes have worn ornate clothing, sat upon the papal throne, and allowed people to kiss their ring. Why, they ask, is there such disparity between the humility of Peter (and Christ, for that matter), and the more grandiose thing that the papacy later became?

Consider this perspective: When an ambassador is representing his country abroad, should he wear a tee-shirt and jeans, or formal attire? When he's taking part in official diplomatic ceremonies, are the marks of honor given the ambassador by his host country signs of respect for him personally or for the country he represents? In like manner, the pope is the primary ambassador for Christ and for the heavenly kingdom. Formal attire honors the dignity of his office and the divine Person he represents. Marks of honor given the pope are not for him personally, but for Jesus. Each pope must recognize this, and humbly acknowledge the seeming paradox that he is both a lowly sinner and the Vicar of Christ.

What about the allegedly lavish riches of the Church? Shouldn't the pope follow the scriptural example of humility, sell all the valuable items in the Vatican's possession, and give the proceeds to the poor? After all, Jesus said, "If you would be perfect, go, sell what you possess and give to the poor, and you will have treasure in heaven" (Matt. 19:21).

On the surface this might seem like a convincing argument. However, the pope and the Vatican are quite unique in the world. There are times when an item's value surpasses what it can be sold for. There are times when its "highest and best use" is not to simply cash it to alleviate some temporal suffering. Consider the elaborate beauty of the temple in ancient Israel (see 1 Kings 6), built according to God's command. Also consider this Bible passage:

Six days before the Passover, Jesus came to Bethany, where Lazarus was, whom Jesus had raised from the dead. There they made him a supper; Martha served, and Lazarus was one of those at table with him. Mary took a pound of costly ointment of pure nard, and anointed the feet of Jesus and wiped his feet with her hair; and the house was filled with the fragrance of the ointment. But Judas Iscariot, one of his disciples (he who was to betray him), said, "Why was this ointment not sold for three hundred denarii and given to the poor?" This he said, not that he cared for the poor, but because he was a thief, and as he had the money box he used to take what was put into it. Jesus said, "Let her alone, let her keep it for the day of my burial. The poor you always have with you, but you do not always have me." (John 12:1–8)

Thus, valuable items are sometimes best used for the glorification of God. Like the ointment in this passage, Vatican assets (such as they are; we should be careful in our assumptions about the degree of the Church's wealth, which is less than many think) are put to use for the glory of God, not the pope. People throughout the world have access to them when they visit the Vatican. If they were to be sold, the poor of the world might benefit for a very short time. But if they remain the property of the Church, they can be used to give glory to God indefinitely. In maintaining such practices, then, popes are not rejecting Christ's humble example.

9. Did Christians in the early Church recognize Peter as head of the apostles?

As with his presence in Rome, when we examine the writings of the Church Fathers and other early Christians, we discover ample attestation to his primacy among the apostles.

Clement of Alexandria (200): "[Peter is] the chosen, the preeminent, the first among the disciples, for whom alone with himself the Savior paid the tribute."[25]

Tertullian (211): "[R]emember that the Lord left the keys of [heaven] to Peter here, and through him to the Church."[26]

Letter of Clement to James (221): "Be it known to you, my lord, that Simon [Peter], who, for the sake of the true faith, and the most sure foundation of his doctrine, was set apart to be the foundation of the Church, and for this end was by Jesus himself, with his truthful mouth, named Peter, the first fruits of our Lord, the first of the apostles; to whom first the Father revealed the Son; whom the Christ, with good reason, blessed; the called, and elect."[27]

Origen (248): "[I]f we were to attend carefully to the Gospels, we should also find, in relation to those things which seem to be common to Peter . . . a great difference and a preeminence in the things [Jesus] said to Peter, compared with the second class [of apostles]."[28]

Cyprian of Carthage (251): "[A] primacy is given to Peter, whereby it is made clear that there is but one Church and one chair."[29]

Cyril of Jerusalem (350): "[Peter is] the first and foremost of the apostles" and "both the chief of the apostles and the keeper of the keys of the kingdom of heaven."[30]

Ephraim the Syrian (351), writing as Christ to Peter: "You are the head of the fountain from which my teaching flows; you are the chief of my disciples. . . . I have chosen you to be, as it were, the firstborn in my institution so that, as the heir, you may be executor of my treasures."[31]

Jerome (393): "[O]ne among the twelve is chosen to be their head in order to remove any occasion for division."[32] Jerome also, in 396, calls Peter, "chief of the apostles."[33]

Augustine (411): "Among these [apostles] Peter alone almost everywhere deserved to represent the whole Church. Because of that representation of the Church, which only he bore, he deserved to hear 'I will give to you the keys of the kingdom of heaven.'"[34] He also made note a few years later, in 415, of: "the primacy which he [Peter] bore among the disciples";[35] and then in 416, attests that: "the first of the apostles is the most blessed Peter."[36]

Council of Ephesus (431): "[T]he head of the whole Faith, the head of the apostles, is blessed Peter the apostle,"[37] and "[Peter is] prince and head of the apostles, pillar of the Faith, and foundation of the Catholic Church."[38]

Pope Leo I (445): "Our Lord Jesus Christ . . . has placed the principal charge on the blessed Peter, chief of all the apostles, and from him as from the head wishes his gifts to flow to all the body"[39] He added, "[A]mong the most blessed apostles, though they were alike in honor, there was a certain distinction of power. All were equal in being chosen, but it was given to one to be preeminent over the others."[40]

These examples and others show that the earliest Christians did, indeed, recognize Peter's primacy among the apostles. Moreover, this appears to have been an undisputed fact, because there are no examples of Christians in the early centuries *denying* Peter's primacy—or, for that matter, the succession of other bishops of Rome to the Petrine office.

10. Are Peter's papal successors foretold in the Bible?

Scripture does not explicitly mention who Peter's successors would be, but the Bible does provide evidence of apostolic succession in general from the earliest days of the Church. We first see this taking place when Judas, having betrayed the Lord and committed suicide, is succeeded by Matthias. Peter addresses the other apostles in the Upper Room:

"For it is written in the book of Psalms, 'Let his habitation become desolate, and let there be no one to live in it'; and 'His office let another take.' So one of the men who have accompanied us during all the time that the Lord Jesus went in and out among us, beginning from the baptism of John until the day when he was taken up from us—one of these men must become with us a witness to his resurrection." And they put forward two, Joseph called Barsabbas, who was surnamed Justus, and Matthias. And they prayed and said, "Lord, who knowest the hearts of all men, show which one of these two thou hast chosen to take the place in this ministry and apostleship from which Judas turned aside, to go to his own place." And they cast lots for them, and the lot fell on Matthias; and he was enrolled with the eleven apostles. (Acts 1:20–26)

Thus, Matthias was chosen to succeed Judas. The apostles never thought, however, that their own number was to be limited to twelve, nor that the number of their successors was limited. And thus St. Paul, who was appointed to be an apostle by Jesus after the Ascension, went on to appoint multiple bishops—successors of the apostles—to carry on his work (see Acts 9). St. Timothy was one such successor. To him, Paul writes, "[W]hat you have heard from me before many witnesses entrust to faithful men who will be able to teach others also" (2 Tim. 2:2). Here it is easy to see that Paul is passing on the authority he received from Jesus to Timothy, who would then go on to appoint further successors, who would go on to do the same (and so on). He writes similarly to Titus: "This is why I left you in Crete, that you might amend what was defected, and appoint elders in every town as I directed you" (Titus 1:5).

Paul recognized apostolic succession to be a gift handed on through a special ritual. He wrote to Timothy: "Do not neglect the gift you have, which was given you by prophetic utterance when the elders laid their hands upon you" (1 Tim. 4:14). Here, Paul writes of Timothy's ordination, through which he received the sacrament of holy orders. This is the special way that bishops are appointed. It makes sense that such a formal rite would be instituted in order to preserve authentic succession of authority, especially concerning matters of faith and morals, thereby ensuring the unity Jesus desires. This rite is the Catholic sacrament of holy orders.

No one can give himself the mandate and the mission to proclaim the gospel. The one sent by the Lord does not speak and act on his own authority, but by virtue of Christ's authority; not as a member of the community, but speaking to it in the name of Christ. No one can bestow grace on himself; it must be given and offered. This fact presupposes ministers of grace, authorized and empowered by Christ. . . . The ministry in which Christ's emissaries do and give by God's grace what they cannot do and give by their own powers, is called a "sacrament" by the Church's tradition. Indeed, the ministry of the Church is conferred by a special sacrament. (CCC 875)

Papal succession is similar to apostolic succession, but also different in that most popes down through the history of the Church were ordained bishops before being selected to succeed Peter in his papal office. The process of electing a new successor has taken various forms over time. Today, and over the past 700-plus years, popes are selected through a process known as the *conclave*. The term is a Latin noun meaning a room that can be locked. Papal successors are elected in such a room (today it's the Sistine Chapel), usually by and from among the highest-ranking bishops of the Church.

In the interregnum between the death of one pope and the election of a new one, the day-to-day business of the Church is administered by the cardinal *camerlengo* (Latin for chamberlain). The *camerlengo* only handles matters of immediate urgency, however; all other matters are postponed until a new pope is elected.

If a pope were to resign from his papal office (as Benedict XVI did in 2013), he would retain his sacramental powers as bishop, but the special powers and authority unique to the papal office would pass to his successor, as those properly belong to the office of the papacy and not to the person holding that office.

11. Did Christians in the early Church recognize the authority of St. Peter's papal successors in Rome?

As with Peter's primacy, the Church Fathers and other early Christian writers not only recognized Peter's papal successors in Rome to be the authoritative leaders of the one Church founded by Jesus—they did so unanimously. Here are some examples.

Ignatius of Antioch (A.D. 110), writing to the Church in Rome: "[Y]ou hold the presidency in love, named after Christ and named after the Father."[41] Later, he added, "I desire only that what you have enjoined in your instructions may remain in force."[42]

Dionysius of Corinth (170): "Today we have observed the Lord's holy day, in which we have read your letter [Pope Soter]. Whenever we do read it, we shall be able to profit thereby, as also we do when we read the earlier letter written to us by [Pope] Clement."[43]

St. Irenaeus (189): "But since it would be too long to enumerate in such a volume as this the succession of all the churches, we shall confound all those who, in whatever manner, whether through self-satisfaction or vainglory, or through blindness and wicked opinion, assemble other than where it is proper, by pointing out here the successions of the bishops of the greatest and most ancient church known to all, founded and organized at Rome by the two most glorious apostles, Peter and Paul, that church which has the tradition and the faith which comes down to us after having been announced to men by the apostles. With that church, because of its superior origin, all the churches must agree, that is, all the faithful in the whole world, and it is in her that the faithful everywhere have maintained the apostolic tradition."[44]

Cyprian of Carthage (253), to Pope Cornelius in Rome: "We decided to send and are sending a letter to you from all throughout the province [where we are] so that all our colleagues might give their decided approval and support to you and to your communion, that is, to both the unity and the charity of the Catholic Church."[45]

Firmilian (253): "[Pope] Stephen . . . boasts of the place of his episcopate, and contends that he holds the succession from Peter, on whom the foundations of the Church were laid. . . . Stephen . . . announces that he holds by succession the throne of Peter."[46]

Pope Julius I (341): "Are you ignorant that the custom has been to write first to us and then for a just decision to be passed from this place [Rome]? . . . What I write about this is for the common good. For what we have heard from the blessed apostle Peter, these things I signify to you."[47]

Optatus (367): "[I]n the city of Rome the episcopal chair was given first to Peter; the chair in which Peter sat, the same who was head—that is why he is also called Cephas [Rock]—of all the apostles, the one chair in which unity is maintained by all. Neither do the apostles proceed individually on their own, and anyone who would [presume to] set up another chair in opposition to that single chair would, by that very fact, be a schismatic and a sinner. . . . Recall, then, the origins of your chair, those of you who wish to claim for yourselves the title of holy Church."[48]

Council of Constantinople I (381): "The bishop of Constantinople shall have the primacy of honor after the bishop of Rome, because his city is New Rome."[49]

Pope Damasus I (382): "[T]he holy Roman Church has been placed at the forefront not by the conciliar decisions of other churches, but has received the primacy by the evangelic voice of our Lord and Savior."[50]

Synod of Ambrose (389): "We recognize in the letter of your holiness [Pope Siricius] the vigilance of the good shepherd. You faithfully watch over the gate [of heaven] entrusted to you, and with pious care you guard Christ's sheepfold, you that are worthy to have the Lord's sheep hear and follow you."[51]

Jerome (396), to Pope Damasus I: "I follow no leader but Christ and join in communion with none but your blessedness, that is, with the chair of Peter. I know that this is the rock on which the Church has been built. Whoever eats the Lamb outside this house is profane. Anyone who is not in the ark of Noah will perish when the flood prevails."[52] Later, Jerome added: "He that is joined to the chair of Peter is accepted by me!"[53]

Peter Chrysologus (449): "We exhort you in every respect, honorable brother, to heed obediently what has been written by the most blessed pope of the city of Rome, for blessed Peter, who lives and presides in his own see, provides the truth of faith to those who seek it. For we, by reason of our pursuit of peace and faith, cannot try cases on the faith without the consent of the bishop of Rome."[54]

Council of Chalcedon (451): "We received directions at the hands of the most blessed and apostolic bishop of the Roman city, who is the head of all the churches, which directions say that Dioscorus is not to be allowed to sit in the [present] assembly, but that if he should attempt to take his seat, he is to be cast out. This instruction we must carry out."[55]

Once again, it is quite clear that Christians in the early centuries of the Church recognized yet another important aspect of the papacy: that Peter's papal successors in Rome carry on the papal authority handed on to them through the papal succession. There can really be no doubt that this was the authoritative structure of the Church's hierarchy intended by Jesus from the beginning.

12. Wasn't there more than one pope at times during the Middle Ages?

Sometimes people will argue that there have been periods in Church history when two or three popes were elected and reigned at the same time. This is simply not true. There can be only one pope at a time. It is true, however, that there have been periods when there have been multiple *claimants* to the papacy, sometimes necessitating an official determination of who was actually St. Peter's authentic successor. The so-called *Western Schism* is a prime example of this.

The Western Schism refers to a notorious period during the fourteenth and fifteenth centuries, when the authentic pope was in dispute. Was it the claimant residing in Rome or the one in Avignon, France? It took many decades to resolve.

Due primarily to political reasons, beginning early in the fourteenth century the popes had come to reside in Avignon, but Pope Gregory XI returned the papacy to Rome, where he died in 1378. A conclave in Rome subsequently elected a new pope, who took the name Urban VI. Unfortunately, he quickly fell out of favor with the cardinals who elected him, so later that same year, they elected another pope, who took the name Clement VII and took up residence in Avignon. From the looks of it, it seems that Urban VI had been legitimately elected to the papacy and, since he had not renounced it, Clement VII could not be a valid pope. Even so, a huge disagreement ensued, with an equal number of people recognizing Clement as recognized Urban.

As the disagreement grew over the years, both claimants to the papacy died, and in the late fourteenth century new conclaves attempted to elect new popes to replace them—Boniface IX in Rome and Benedict XIII in Avignon. Boniface IX was subsequently succeeded by Innocent VII and then Gregory XII. Amid the confusion, in 1410 a third claimant to the papacy was elected by a group of cardinals in Pisa, taking the name John XXIII. All three would-be popes claimed support from different regions and nobles of Christendom.

The Council of Constance finally settled the matter in 1414, securing the resignation of the apparently legitimate Pope Gregory XII and the antipope John XXIII, and electing a new pope, who took the name Martin V. Some former adherents to the Avignon papacy continued for a time to support Benedict XIII and his three antipope successors, but none of them would be recognized in history. Since that time, authentic papal succession has been recognized to be the line of claimants following Gregory XI in Rome.

Although Jesus appointed multiple apostles, he appointed only one to be their head. Never has the Church taught that there could be more than one papal successor at a time. Even during the Western Schism, no one thought there was more than one legitimate pope. Rather, the faithful were just divided on precisely who that was. When the air was finally cleared, the matter was settled in a manner that seems quite clear today to historians far removed from the cloud of the political climate of the period.

There will always be a human element in the election and succession of popes, and in certain rare instances over history temporary confusion has resulted from it, but in no way does this undermine the office of the papacy or the principle of Petrine succession.

13. Is there any biblical or historical precedent for the papacy?

As we saw before, Jesus told Peter, "I will give you the keys of the kingdom of heaven, and whatever you bind on earth shall be bound in heaven, and whatever you loose on earth shall be loosed in heaven" (Matt. 16:19). Later on, Jesus gave similar authority to bind and loose to other apostles gathered together as a unit (see Matt. 18:18), but only Peter was given this special authority to act on his own, and only he was given the keys of the kingdom of heaven.

The symbolism of keys was not an innovation introduced by Jesus. We find the same symbolism in ancient Israel when authority was passed from one to another.

For example, the prophet Isaiah foretells that Eliakim will take over the position second in authority to the king of Israel: "I will place on his [Eliakim's] shoulder the key of the house of David; he shall open, and none shall shut; and he shall shut, and none shall open" (Isa. 22:22). In this passage, it is prophesied that Eliakim would essentially be empowered to act on behalf of the king in his absence. Thus, what Jesus told Peter is best understood in a similar way, that Peter would act on Jesus' behalf in his absence (that is, after the Ascension).

Some non-Catholics argue that Revelation 3:7 indicates that Christ is the one who holds the key, not Peter, therefore, Isaiah 22 is a foreshadowing of Christ's coming and *his* authority rather than Peter's. However, it is important to understand that in Isaiah 22 the prophecy is that Eliakim will possess the key of the kingdom not as its *owner*, but as its *steward*, deputed to oversee the king's affairs. If we were to say the same about Christ, then we would falsely conclude that he is merely the king's steward, not the king himself. Of course, we know that Christ is the king himself, the owner of the key, not merely its steward.

Thus, although Jesus is called the holder of the key, he doesn't hold it in the same capacity as Eliakim or he whom Eliakim foreshadows (that is, Peter). As the son of David, Jesus is the heir to the throne. He really *is* the king, not the master of the king's palace, as Eliakim was. As king, Jesus is free to bestow the keys of his kingdom on whomever he wishes without losing the authority those keys represent: he may freely give them to Peter in his absence. This is precisely what Jesus does in Matthew 16:19. Peter has just identified Jesus as the Messiah, which means, among other things, that he acknowledges his kingship. Christ then shows his kingly authority by bestowing on Peter something only the king could give—the keys of the kingdom of heaven. Peter is thus empowered with authority to act on Jesus' behalf while Jesus is away.

Part of this authority is the power to bind and to loose. Again, in ancient Israel, this power was understood as the ability to teach authoritatively, to include or exclude someone from the community, and even to forgive a person's sins. Thus, the pope has supreme authority over the Church community in matters of faith and morals, which includes the charism of infallibility.

The power to "bind and loose" connotes the authority to absolve sins, to pronounce doctrinal judgments, and to make disciplinary decisions in the Church. Jesus entrusted this authority to the Church through the ministry of the apostles and in particular through the ministry of Peter, the only one to whom he specifically entrusted the keys of the kingdom. (CCC 553; see also CCC 1444–45)

A precedent to the pope's ability to teach definitively (that is, the charism of infallibility) may be seen in ancient Israel's chair of Moses. The high priest's authority to speak with the authority of Moses foreshadows the pope's authority to speak with the authority of Christ.

Peter's role in the Church is also somewhat similar to that of the high priest in ancient Israel, who functioned as the earthly leader of God's people. While Christ is the ultimate head of all God's people, he has left Peter and his successors to serve as his visible representatives in his absence.

Thus, Peter was singled out with great authority in the early Church. The other apostles were given similar authority, but only when acting together and in communion with Peter. This continues to apply to their successors as well.

[Jesus] gave [Peter] the keys of his Church and instituted him shepherd of the whole flock. "The office of binding and loosing which was given to Peter was also assigned to the college of apostles united to its head." This pastoral office of Peter and the other apostles belongs to the Church's very foundation and is continued by the bishops under the primacy of the pope. (CCC 881)

Finally, in addition to his special religious powers in the kingdom of God, the pope also serves in a temporal role as an earthly governmental leader. In a real sense, his role mirrors that of King David not only as priest and prophet but also as king. Today he exercises temporal power as the head of the Vatican City state. In earlier centuries the pope often governed much larger domains.

14. What is the charism of infallibility?

Papal infallibility means that the pope is protected from error when he "proclaims by a definitive act a doctrine pertaining to faith or morals" (CCC 891). This does not mean that he is impeccable (incapable of sin) or inerrant (incapable of error).

Christ bestowed the charism of infallibility on St. Peter and his successors. We find evidence of this in Scripture. For example, Jesus told Peter, "Simon, Simon, behold, Satan demanded to have you, that he might sift you like wheat, but I have prayed for you that your faith may not fail; and when you have turned again, strengthen your brethren" (Luke 22:31–32). Interestingly, the Greek word for *you* in the first instance is the plural form— Satan demanded to sift *all* the apostles like wheat. But then Jesus says to Peter, with the singular form of *you,* that he has prayed for him individually, and that he, Peter, would strengthen the other apostles.

As we have seen, early Christians acknowledged Christ's teaching on the primacy of the pope, which involved papal infallibility. But it did not become necessary to infallibly define the doctrine of papal infallibility itself until the First Vatican Council (1869–1870). (Many Catholic doctrines, historically, have not been formally defined until they came into dispute.) People sometimes mistakenly conclude that papal infallibility only came into existence at that time. In reality, it has accompanied the papal office from the beginning, and was simply not something so misunderstood and disputed as to require formal definition, until the nineteenth century.

This question often arises: If a pope gives a statement on an issue that is the complete opposite of the statement of a past pope, which of them is correct?

To answer this, first we must determine whether the statement is a matter of faith and morals. If it is not, popes are free to disagree with each other. If it is, we must determine if one or both of the popes was speaking merely as a private theologian. If one of them was speaking definitively in his capacity as pope, then the presumption of correctness would go to him. We must also consider the possibility that what appears to be a contradiction between a past and present pope may not be. Popes can state the same truth in a variety of ways without contradicting each other. There may also have been theological developments that give new nuances to earlier doctrinal pronouncements.

Truth be told, no pope has ever authoritatively contradicted an earlier pope's infallible statement on a matter of faith and morals. Popes have, however, contradicted (or changed) non-infallible, non-doctrinal decrees of previous popes. To understand how this is possible, it is important to clarify the difference between a doctrine and a discipline.

Every Church discipline is a man-made thing that can be changed as often as the Church desires. This is not to say that the authority to enact discipline is man-made. Keep in mind that the pope's authority to bind and loose includes the authority to make disciplinary decisions in the Church (see CCC 553). As we have seen, the authority to bind and to loose extends far beyond discipline, but it certainly includes the authority to enact discipline as well. Nor should disciplines be enacted without much reason, study, and prudence. Nonetheless, they can be changed to suit the Church's purposes in a given time and place. Examples of disciplines include Lenten fasting and abstinence requirements, the celibate priesthood, and the way the Mass is celebrated (see answer 17 below). Although disciplines are often related to doctrines, they are not matters of doctrine themselves.

A "doctrine," on the other hand, is the teaching of the Church on matters of faith and morals. All such teaching—or at least the basis for it—was handed down to the Church by Jesus and the apostles prior to the death of the last apostle. Scripture refers to doctrine as "the faith which was once for all delivered to the saints" (Jude 1:3). Doctrine can develop over time as the Church comes to understand it better, but it cannot change. No one—not even the pope—has the authority to change doctrine.

That the Church possesses both doctrines and disciplines might seem simple enough on the surface; however, distinguishing between the two is not always a simple task—even when discussing matters with fellow Catholics. This illustrates all the more clearly the need for papal authority!

15. What are *ex cathedra* teachings? Are these the only doctrines Catholics *must* embrace?

Ex cathedra is a Latin phrase that means "from the chair" (that is, the chair of Peter). It refers to the binding and infallible papal teachings promulgated by the pope when, in his capacity as the universal shepherd of the Church, he officially teaches a doctrine on a matter of faith or morals and addresses it to the entire world.

Jesus endorsed this concept as it operated in the Old Testament: "The scribes and the Pharisees sit on Moses' seat [Greek, *cathedras*], so practice and observe whatever they tell you, but not what they do; for they preach, but do not practice" (Matt. 23:2–3). Since Jesus recognized the authority of the Old Testament's teaching authority when it spoke *ex cathedra* (with the authority of Moses), we recognize that the New Testament Magisterium of the Church, which speaks with the authority of Christ (Matt. 10:40, 16:18–19, 18:18; Luke 10:16; 2 Cor. 5:18–20), possesses a binding, infallible teaching power that is guaranteed by Christ (Matt. 28:20; John 14:16, 26, 16:13).

That said, *ex cathedra* teachings are not the only teachings of the pope (or the Church in general) that Catholics must embrace. The Second Vatican Council took great care to point this out:

> This religious submission of mind and will must be shown in a special way to the authentic Magisterium of the Roman Pontiff, even when he is not speaking ex cathedra; that is, it must be shown in such a way that his supreme magisterium is acknowledged with reverence, the judgments made by him are sincerely adhered to, according to his manifest mind and will. His mind and will in the matter may be known either from the character of the documents, from his frequent repetition of the same doctrine, or from his manner of speaking. (LG 25)

This does not mean that Catholics must agree with the mere opinions the pope may voice on matters. It does mean, however, that whatever the pope authentically teaches deserves our assent. The Code of Canon

Law (CIC) mandates this. (Note the authority to bind and to loose is in play here!)

First, the code defines that infallible teachings are those proclaimed as such by the pope as well as those proclaimed by the college of bishops in communion with the pope:

> By virtue of his office, the Supreme Pontiff possesses infallibility in teaching when as the supreme pastor and teacher of all the Christian faithful, who strengthens his brothers and sisters in the faith, he proclaims by definitive act that a doctrine of faith or morals is to be held.
>
> The college of bishops also possesses infallibility in teaching when the bishops gathered together in an ecumenical council exercise the Magisterium as teachers and judges of faith and morals who declare for the universal Church that a doctrine of faith or morals is to be held definitively; or when dispersed throughout the world but preserving the bond of communion among themselves and with the successor of Peter and teaching authentically together with the Roman Pontiff matters of faith or morals, they agree that a particular proposition is to be held definitively. (CIC 749)

No doctrine is understood as defined infallibly unless this is manifestly evident.

Then, the Code defines what teachings a Catholic must assent to as well as the degree of assent required:

A person must believe with divine and Catholic faith all those things contained in the word of God, written or handed on, that is, in the one deposit of faith entrusted to the Church, and at the same time proposed as divinely revealed either by the solemn Magisterium of the Church or by its ordinary and universal magisterium which is manifested by the common adherence of the Christian faithful under the leadership of the sacred magisterium; therefore all are bound to avoid any doctrines whatsoever contrary to them.

Each and every thing which is proposed definitively by the magisterium of the Church concerning the doctrine of faith and morals, that is, each and every thing which is required to safeguard reverently and to expound faithfully the same deposit of faith, is also to be firmly embraced and retained; therefore, one who rejects those propositions which are to be held definitively is opposed to the doctrine of the Catholic Church. (CIC 750)

Thus, all the doctrines of the Magisterium, not just those that come *ex cathedra* from the pope, are backed by Christ's own authority and deserve the assent[56] of every faithful Catholic.

16. Didn't Pope Paul VI and the Second Vatican Council contradict previous popes regarding the doctrine of "no salvation outside the Church"?

One of the most misunderstood teachings of the Catholic Church is this one: "Outside the Church there is no salvation" (*extra ecclesiam nulla salus*).

Those trying to grasp the meaning of this teaching often struggle with its formulations by various popes and councils down through history. They usually begin by quoting the formulation of the doctrine promulgated in 1215 by Lateran Council IV under Pope Innocent III: "There is indeed one universal Church of the faithful, outside of which nobody at all is saved." They will then move on to Pope Boniface VIII's 1302 papal bull *Unam Sanctam,* which states: "Now, therefore, we declare, say, determine and pronounce that for every human creature it is necessary for salvation to be subject to the authority of the Roman pontiff." Finally, they will likely quote the 1441 Council of Florence under Pope Eugene IV, which states that the Church "firmly believes, professes, and preaches that none of those who are outside of the Catholic Church, not only pagans, but also Jews, heretics, and schismatics, can become sharers of eternal life."

Believing that they fully understand these statements, they compare them to a 1964 statement in the Second Vatican Council's document *Lumen Gentium,* promulgated by Pope Paul VI: "Those also can attain to salvation who through no fault of their own do not know the Gospel of Christ or His Church, yet sincerely seek God and moved by grace strive by their deeds to do His will as it is known to them through the dictates of conscience" (LG 16).

With such isolated information it's easy to suspect that Pope Paul VI contradicted the statements of the prior popes. Some people rashly and mistakenly conclude that papal infallibility has been compromised. Of course, to understand an isolated formulation of any Church teaching, one must study the historical context within which it was written—why it was written, what was going on in the Church at the time, who the intended audience was, and so on. One must also discover how the Magisterium understands its own teaching. If we fail to do this and choose instead to treat a particular formulation as a stand-alone teaching, we run the risk of seriously misunderstanding it.

As it turns out, by the time Vatican II came about, the Church recognized that its formal teaching about the necessity of the Catholic Church for salvation was already being widely misunderstood, so the council rearticulated this teaching in a more positive way. The *Catechism* begins to address this whole topic with this statement (CCC 846): "How are we to understand this affirmation, often repeated by the Church Fathers? Reformulated positively, it means that all salvation

56

comes from Christ the Head through the Church which is his Body." It then goes on to quote *Lumen Gentium*:

> Basing itself on Scripture and Tradition, the council teaches that the Church, a pilgrim now on earth, is necessary for salvation: the one Christ is the mediator and the way of salvation; he is present to us in his body which is the Church. He himself explicitly asserted the necessity of faith and baptism, and thereby affirmed at the same time the necessity of the Church which men enter through baptism as through a door. Hence they could not be saved who, knowing that the Catholic Church was founded as necessary by God through Christ, would refuse either to enter it or to remain in it. (LG 14)

This sounds quite similar to the teaching of the prior popes. But then the *Catechism* elaborates further:

This affirmation is not aimed at those who, through no fault of their own, do not know Christ and his Church:

> Those who, through no fault of their own, do not know the Gospel of Christ or his Church, but who nevertheless seek God with a sincere heart, and, moved by grace, try in their actions to do his will as they know it through the dictates of their conscience—those too may achieve eternal salvation. (CCC 847, LG 16)

This clarifies how the Magisterium has always understood this teaching: no one goes to hell through no fault of his own. Although it is normatively necessary to be a Catholic to be saved, there are exceptions that the prior popes' statements do not explicitly state yet that were always implicitly understood.

This teaching is consistent with Jesus' own teaching about those who innocently reject him: "If I had not come and spoken to them, they would not have sin" (John 15:22). But once a person comes to know the truth, he must embrace it or he will be culpable of rejecting it. We see this in Jesus' words to the Pharisees: "If you were blind, you would have no guilt; but now that you say, 'We see,' your guilt remains" (John 9:41). Paul taught likewise concerning the Gentiles (Rom. 2:14–16):

> When Gentiles who have not the law do by nature what the law requires, they are a law to themselves, even though they do not have the law. They show that what the law requires is written on their hearts, while their conscience also bears witness and their conflicting thoughts accuse or perhaps excuse them on that day when, according to my gospel, God judges the secrets of men by Christ Jesus.

Notice Paul's carefully chosen words: "their conflicting thoughts accuse or perhaps excuse them." Paul did not say that those who are innocently ignorant of the truth will be saved; he simply keeps open the possibility of it. Similarly, he wrote: "[I]s God the God of Jews only? Is he not the God of Gentiles also? Yes, of Gentiles also, since God is one; and he will justify the circumcised on the ground of their faith and the uncircumcised through their faith" (Rom. 3:29–30).

Thus, it is possible in some circumstances for people to be saved who have not been fully initiated into the Catholic Church. Pope Paul VI did not change this doctrine at Vatican II. Papal infallibility has not been compromised.

17. Can the pope infallibly bind all future popes to a specific liturgical discipline?

As we noted earlier, by its very nature a discipline is a changeable practice that is determined by those with the authority to impose it. Dogma, on the other hand, is a definition of objective supernatural reality and therefore cannot be changed.

The Code of Canon Law says this about the authority of the pope:

The bishop of the Roman Church, in whom continues the office given by the Lord uniquely to Peter, the first of the Apostles, and to be transmitted to his successors, is the head of the college of bishops, the Vicar of Christ, and the pastor of the universal

Church on earth. By virtue of his office he possesses supreme, full, immediate, and universal ordinary power in the Church, which he is always able to exercise freely. (CIC 331)

"Supreme, full, immediate, and universal ordinary power" includes disciplinary authority. If a preceding pope could hamstring the disciplinary authority of his successors by issuing a disciplinary decree binding upon his successors under pain of mortal sin, then the current pope could not be said to have full disciplinary authority over the Church.

The disciplinary authority of a particular pope ends with his death. Successors may choose to continue to promulgate the disciplinary edicts of their predecessors because such edicts continue to be of importance to the life of the Church, but they are not bound to do so.

This question often arises in the context of the changes to the way the Mass is celebrated that were promulgated by Pope Paul VI in the late 1960s after the Second Vatican Council. There are some today who question the pope's authority to institute the liturgical changes he did; they claim that in 1570, Pope St. Pius V defined certain elements of the Mass's celebration as doctrine. Pius V's directives were promulgated "in perpetuity" and are said by some to be unchangeable doctrine.

But Pius V's Apostolic Constitution *Quo Primum* concerned disciplinary matters, not teachings on faith or morals. Evidence of this is that teaching on faith or morals would not—indeed, could not—allow for the exceptions named in *Quo Primum,* such as "unless approval of the practice of saying Mass differently was given" or "unless there has prevailed a custom of a similar kind" or "We in no wise rescind their above-mentioned prerogative or custom." Such matters of Church discipline always remain subject to future change by equal or greater authority. In light of this, wording such as "in perpetuity" must be understood as "from now on, until this or another equal or greater authority determines otherwise." Paul VI certainly held equal authority to Pius V. Therefore, changes to the Mass under his authority were licit and valid and were an example of disciplinary changes, not doctrinal changes.

18. What other challenges to papal infallibility are there?

Some assert that papal infallibility is not truly certain, and as proof they cite the case of Pope Zozimus, who is said to have pronounced the arch-heretic Pelagius to be orthodox and then later reversed his pronouncement.

Pelagius was a fifth-century monk who denied original sin and taught that God's grace was not necessary for the performance of good works, and thus for salvation. Zozimus (r. 417–418) was approached by

Pelagius's follower Caelestius, who brought a profession of faith from Pelagius for the pope's examination. Zozimus examined Caelestius and the profession and found nothing heretical in them. He said the African bishops, who had condemned Pelagius and Caelestius, had been hasty, and he instructed Africans with charges against them to appear in Rome for further investigation.

This prompted outrage among the African bishops, since they considered the Pelagian controversy to have been closed by Zozimus's predecessor, Innocent I. Zozimus responded by stressing the primacy of the Roman see and by explaining to them that he had not settled the matter definitively and that he did not intend to do so without consulting them. He said that his predecessor's decision remained in effect until he had finished investigating the matter.

The bishops provided Zozimus with additional evidence against Pelagius, and after reviewing it the pope condemned Pelagianism. His initial assessment had been a tentative judgment, based on partial evidence. He did not issue a definitive judgment, much less a doctrinal definition, as indicated by the fact he asked for additional evidence to be sent to Rome. Therefore, the case of Zozimus does not really touch on the doctrine of papal infallibility.

Another challenge asserts that Cardinal John Henry Newman, the popular Anglican convert from the nineteenth-century Oxford Movement, rejected the doctrine of papal infallibility until its definition at the First Vatican Council and only accepted it out of obedience afterward.

This is actually not true. Cardinal Newman professed that he personally believed that the pope must be infallible, but he questioned the issuing of a formal definition of the doctrine at that particular time. He was not alone among the Church hierarchy in holding this opinion and was perfectly within his rights to do so. Once the definition was issued he embraced it unhesitatingly.

A further challenge is the modern claim that the Second Vatican Council did away with all the stress on the pope as an infallible teacher. Do Vatican II writings say this?

There is no Vatican II document that "did away with" papal infallibility. Vatican II actually reaffirmed, in no uncertain terms, the teaching of Vatican I on papal authority. *Lumen Gentium* says this:

[A]ll this teaching about the institution, the perpetuity, the meaning and reason for the sacred primacy of the Roman Pontiff and of his infallible magisterium, this Sacred Council again proposes to be firmly believed by all the faithful. Continuing in that same undertaking, this Council is resolved to declare and proclaim before all men the doctrine concerning bishops, the successors of the apostles, who together with the successor of Peter, the Vicar of Christ, the visible Head of the whole Church, govern the house of the living God. (LG 18)

Thus, Vatican II restated Vatican I's teaching on the papacy, but also sketched out the role of bishops in the Church. Bishops as teachers and pastors acting in union with the pope are said to be acting according to the principle of collegiality. There is a renewed stress on the pope as head of a college of bishops, but there is nothing that subordinates the pope to this college. In no sense can Vatican II be taken as "doing away with" papal authority as previously defined.

19. Should the pope be called "Holy Father"? According to the Bible, only God is holy and only God is our Father.

People sometimes wonder why Catholics refer to the pope as the "Holy Father" and they ask for a rational explanation for this apparent blasphemy.

Only God is holy by his very essence; however, a person, place, or thing can be holy by virtue of association with God. To call something holy is to express the idea of consecration—that someone or something belongs to God. That is why the Bible calls many persons, places, and things holy.

In Exodus 3:5, the ground on which Moses stands is called "holy." In Exodus 19:6, God tells the Israelites through Moses, "and you shall be to me a kingdom of priests and a holy nation." God's dwelling place in the Tabernacle is "holy" (Exod. 28:43), as is the city of Jerusalem (Isa. 48:2). Even a goat, the victim of sacrifice to God, is called "holy" in Leviticus 10:17.

In the New Testament, John the Baptist is called "holy" (Mark 6:20). After Christ's death and Resurrection, Christ's followers are referred to as "holy" (Eph. 1:4; 5:27; Col. 1:22; 3:12; Heb. 3:1). In 1 Peter 1:16 we read, "it is written, 'You shall be holy, for I am holy.'" The apostles are called "holy" (Eph. 3:5) and bishops are called to be "holy" as well (Titus 1:8).

Since we are his holy people, and his people are the Church, it is fitting that the head of his holy people be called Holy Father—not because of his own merit, but because Christ died for him and for the Church that he leads on earth.

But what about calling the pope (or anyone else, for that matter) "Father"? Didn't Jesus forbid this when he said, "[C]all no man your father on earth, for you have one Father, who is in heaven"? (Matt. 23:9).

First, let's consider the use of the term *father* in general. Common sense tells us that Jesus wasn't forbidding us to use the word to refer to our male biological parent. In fact, to forbid this would rob the term of its meaning when applied to God, for there would no longer be any earthly counterpart for the analogy of divine Fatherhood. The concept of God's role as Father would be meaningless if we obliterated the concept of earthly fatherhood.

Some other applications of the term seem to be equally allowable. The Church's practice in the apostolic age evidences this. For example, in Acts 7:2, Stephen refers to "our father Abraham," and in Romans 9:10, Paul speaks of "our forefather Isaac." There are also numerous examples in the New Testament of *father* being used as a form of address and reference, even for men who are not biologically related to the speaker. Some individuals genuinely have a spiritual fatherhood, meaning that they can be referred to as spiritual fathers. For example, Paul wrote of himself, "I became your father in Christ Jesus through the gospel" (1 Cor. 4:–15).

Jesus is clearly using hyperbole when he says not to call anyone our father, or else we wouldn't be able to refer to our earthly fathers as such. It doesn't seem that he was forbidding the acknowledgement of spiritual fatherhood, because we see that acknowledgement elsewhere in Scripture. So what use did Jesus intend to forbid?

Ultimately, God is our supreme protector, provider, and instructor. His fatherhood is of a singular kind. Jesus, then, is warning us *not to attribute that particular kind or degree of fatherhood to anyone but God*. We must not give either our natural or our spiritual fathers the filial devotion due to God alone.

This bring us to the pope. There is not only legitimate cause for recognizing him as a spiritual father but also an Old Testament precedent for doing so. Consider again the foreshadowing of the papacy prophesied in Isaiah 22. Of Eliakim, an Old Testament type of (or precursor to) the pope, it is prophesied, "he shall be a father to the inhabitants of Jerusalem and to the house of Judah" (Isa. 22:21). If Eliakim, the king of Jerusalem's vicar, was to be Israel's father, how much more so is the pope, Christ's vicar, the Church's "Father"?

Thus, not only may the pope be referred to as holy and be recognized as our spiritual father, it is legitimate and biblically sound to call him *Holy Father*.

20. Was there once a female pope named Joan?

Accounts of a "popess" named Joan occasionally captivate the media and popular imagination, but they are nothing more than mere fiction. The myth is often used against the Church, however, in an attempt to discredit the papacy. If such a farce were to be true, it would seem to make a mockery of the papal office and even discredit its authenticity.

One version of the infamous fable goes something like this: A deceitful woman disguised herself as a man and worked her way up through the ranks of the hierarchy of the Church. She eventually became pope sometime around the beginning of the twelfth century. Then, one day as she took part in a papal procession on horseback, she suddenly gives birth to a son, exposing her deception and bringing embarrassment to the papacy and the Church. The mob then dragged her through the city behind a horse, stoned her to death, and buried her on the spot.

This rendering of the story dates back to the thirteenth century writings of papal chronicler Jean de Mailly, a Dominican friar. Even so, it is seriously lacking in any verifiable details—not even her name is provided—and there is simply no outside evidence lending credence to it whatsoever.

Another, more detailed, version of the story, also from the thirteenth century, dates the absurd occurrence much earlier, to just after the papacy of Leo IV in the ninth century, coinciding with the reign of Benedict III (855–858). According to this rendition, a bright, studious young girl disguised as a boy named John of Mainz studied in Athens and went on to became a teacher in Rome. There she earned the respect of scholars, and the hierarchy of the Church eventually elevated her to the papacy. Similar to the other version of the story, she is said to have given birth during a papal procession; however, subsequent details are sketchy. It is not clear whether she died soon after her deception was uncovered or if she survived and was made to do penance for several years. Her son, the story concludes grew up to become a bishop in the Church.

The details of this rendition of the fable are credited to papal chaplain Martin of Troppau, also a Dominican friar and chronicler of papal history. However, there is no evidence to corroborate this presentation of the story either, and, in fact, there is one telling piece of evidence to refute it: A coin minted during the reign of Benedict III testifies to the authenticity of *his* reign during the period in question and exposes the pure fantasy of the supposed popess.

Other versions of the fable developed over the years. However, there exists no evidence at all for any account's veracity. On the contrary, all are quite suspicious. For one thing, the earliest known account did not arise until long after the supposed occurrence of the events—whether that be in the ninth or the twelfth century. Surely if there was any truth to such a fantastical story, there would be some evidence for it much closer to the period when it actually happened. Additionally, no other credible papal histories provide any reliable account whatsoever of Joan's existence. Historical records *do* provide evidence of who the popes actually were over the history of the Church—including those from around the times of Joan's purported existence—that refute the reign of any such claimant to the papacy.

Simply put, despite the story's hold on the popular imagination and frequent repetition in anti-Catholic literature, there are no facts—from either Catholic or secular sources—to support it, and there is ample evidence to refute it.

Finally, it should be noted that there could not ever *actually* have been a Popess Joan—or any other female pope for that matter. The successor to Peter's chair is the highest level of the Church's earthly ministerial priesthood, infallibly defined as a male-only priesthood. Pope John Paul II confirmed this doctrine in his 1994 apostolic letter *Ordinatio Sacerdotalis*, and the Congregation for the Doctrine of the Faith subsequently affirmed its certitude. Indeed, as the highest office of the priesthood, the pope is the vicar of Christ, Jesus' visible representative on earth. Just as Jesus was and is a man, so must be his vicar.

About the Author

Jim Blackburn is a Catholic apologist, speaker, and writer. He holds a master's degree in Theology from John Paul the Great Catholic University and is the author of the book *101 Quick Questions with Catholic Answers: Marriage, Divorce, and Annulment.* Jim supervised the Catholic Answers Q&A department for many years and he remains a regular guest on the *Catholic Answers Live* radio program.

Endnotes

1   *Demurrer Against the Heretics* 22.

2   *Modesty* 21:9–10.

3   *Letter of Clement to James* 2.

4   *Clementine Homilies* 17:19.

5   *Homilies on Exodus* 5:4.

6   *The Unity of the Catholic Church* 4; 1st edition.

7   *Letters* 43[40]:5.

8   *Letters* 66[69]:8.

9   Collected in Cyprian's *Letters* 74[75]:17.

10 *Homilies* 4:1.

11 *The Schism of the Donatists* 2:2.

12 *The Faith* 4:5.

13 *Against Jovinian* 1:26.

14 *Against Heresies* 3:3:3.

15 *Demurrer Against the Heretics* 32:2.

16 Eusebius, *Church History* 5:28:3.

17 *Letters* 55:[52]:8.

18 *Church History* 3:4:9–10.

19 *The Schism of the Donatists* 2:2.

20 *Medicine Chest Against All Heresies* 27:6.

21 *Decree of Damasus* 3.

22 *Against the Luciferians* 23.

23 *Against the Letters of Petilani* 2:118.

24 *Letters* 25:2.

25 *Who Is the Rich Man That Is Saved?* 21:3–5.

26 *Antidote Against the Scorpion* 10.

27 *Letter of Clement to James* 2.

28 *Commentary on Matthew* 13:31.

29 *The Unity of the Catholic Church* 4; 1st edition.

30 *Catechetical Lectures* 2:19.

31 *Homilies* 4:1.

32 *Against Jovinian* 1:26.

33 *Lives of Illustrious Men* 1.

34 *Sermons* 295:2.

35 *Commentary on Psalm 108* 1.

36 *Commentary on John* 56:1.

37 *Acts of the Council,* session 2.

38 Ibid., session 3.

39 *Letters* 10:1.

40 *Letters* 14:11.

41 *Letter to the Romans* 1:1.

42 Ibid., 3:1.

43 *Letter to Pope Soter* in Eusebius, *Church History* 4:23:9.

44 *Against Heresies* 3:3:2.

45 *Letters* 48:1, 3.

46 Collected in Cyprian's *Letters* 74[75]:17.

47 *Letter on Behalf of Athanasius* , in Athanasius, *Apology Against the Arians* 20–35.

48 *The Schism of the Donatists* 2:2.

49 Canon 3.

50 *Decree of Damasus* 3.

51 *Synodal Letter to Pope Siricius.*

52 *Letters* 15:2.

53 Ibid., 16:2.

54 *Letters* 25:2.

55 *Acts of the Council*, session 1.

56 This can be the "assent of faith," which is due to infallible teachings of the Magisterium, or "religious assent," which is due to propositions from the Magisterium that are aimed at a better understanding of Catholic faith or morals, but which are not definitively offered as infallible. See CCC 892.